Creative Education

MAMMALS

PART ONE

On The Cover:
A Sabretooth Cat.
After the dinosaurs died out,
wonderful mammals evolved to
take their places.
Cover Art by Walter Stuart.

Published by Creative Education, Inc., 123 South Broad Street, Mankato, Minnesota 56001

Printed by permission of Wildlife Education, Ltd.

ISBN 0-88682-395-1

Created and written by
John Bonnett Wexo

Chief Artist
Walter Stuart

Senior Art Consultant
Mark Hallett

Design Consultant
Eldon Paul Slick

Production Art Director
Maurene Mongan

Production Artists
Bob Meyer
Fiona King
Hildago Ruiz

Photo Staff
Renee C. Burch
Katharine Boskoff

Publisher
Kenneth Kitson

Associate Publisher
Ray W. Ehlers

MAMMALS

PART ONE

This Volume is Dedicated to: Bob Sheehan, Sal Tarrango and all of my other friends at Frye & Smith in San Diego. Their unfailing professionalism and high craftsmanship show on every page of every book.

Art Credits

Pages Eight and Nine: Barbara Hoopes-Ambler; Page Ten: Left and Upper Right, Walter Stuart; Pages Ten and Eleven: Center, Barbara Hoopes-Ambler; Page Eleven: Upper Left, Robert Bampton; Upper Middle, Upper Right and Middle, Walter Stuart; Page Twelve: Middle Left and Upper Right, Barbara Hoopes-Ambler; Lower Left, Robert Bampton; Pages Twelve and Thirteen: Upper Center, Robert Bampton; Lower Center, Barbara Hoopes-Ambler; Page Thirteen: Upper Left and Middle Right, Barbara Hoopes-Ambler; Upper Right and Lower Left, Robert Bampton; Page Fourteen: Left and Right, Walter Stuart; Pages Fourteen and Fifteen: Barbara Hoopes-Ambler; Page Fifteen: Upper Left and Lower Right, Walter Stuart; Middle Right, Robert Bampton; Page Sixteen: Middle Left, Robert Bampton; Lower Right, Walter Stuart; Pages Sixteen and Seventeen: Barbara Hoopes-Ambler; Page Seventeen: Middle Left, Robert Bampton; Lower Right, Walter Stuart; Page Eighteen: Lower Middle, Robert Bampton; Pages Eighteen and Nineteen: Barbara Hoopes-Ambler; Page Nineteen: Upper Right and Lower Left, Robert Bampton; Page Twenty: Upper Left, Walter Stuart; Middle Right, Lower Left and Lower Right, Robert Bampton; Pages Twenty and Twenty-one: Barbara Hoopes-Ambler; Page Twenty-one: Upper Left, Upper Right and Middle Right, Robert Bampton; Lower Right, Walter Stuart; Pages Twenty-two and Twenty-three: Background, Timothy Hayward; Figures, Chuck Byron.

Photographic Credits

Pages Six and Seven: Gordon Menzie (Model by Andrea von Sholly); Page Eleven: Lower Right, Jane Burton (Bruce Coleman, Ltd.); Page Twenty-one: Upper Left, Joe McDonald (Animals Animals).

Creative Education would like to thank Wildlife Education, Ltd., for granting them the right to print and distribute this hardbound edition.

Contents

The dinosaurs were gone—and the mammals were ready to take over.

BOOK NINE

Mammals
Part One

For more than 130 million years, the mammals lived "in the shadow" of the dinosaurs. During that incredibly long time, they were forced to be **nocturnal animals**—so they developed bodies that could live in the cold and dark of the night. Their hair grew longer, their eyesight got better, they evolved special kinds of teeth. Then, about 65 million years ago, **the dinosaurs died out**— and the way was open for **the mammals** to "take over the earth."

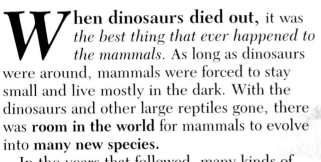

When dinosaurs died out, it was *the best thing that ever happened to the mammals.* As long as dinosaurs were around, mammals were forced to stay small and live mostly in the dark. With the dinosaurs and other large reptiles gone, there was **room in the world** for mammals to evolve into **many new species.**

In the years that followed, many kinds of mammals evolved to fill niches that used to belong to dinosaurs and other reptiles. After millions of years, almost all of the large animals on earth were mammals. The Age of the dinosaurs was over. **The Age of the Mammals** was beginning!

To find food and survive in their new niches, mammals evolved bodies that were often **similar to the reptiles** they replaced. For example, bulky dinosaurs with horns were replaced by bulky mammals with horns.

REPTILE

Pterosaurs died out and the **bats replaced them.** Like the pterosaurs, bats had wings of skin.

MAMMAL

Large plant-eating dinosaurs with long necks were replaced by large plant-eating mammals **with trunks.** The trunks worked like long necks to reach food.

MAMMAL

MAMMAL

REPTILE

MAMMAL

Meat-eating dinosaurs with claws and sharp teeth were replaced by meat-eating mammals with claws and sharp teeth.

REPTILE

REPTILE

In the ocean, marine reptiles with sleek bodies and sharp teeth died out. They were replaced by mammals with sleek bodies and sharp teeth.

MAMMAL

9

Mammals took over so many niches because they had bodies and types of behavior that gave them **special advantages.** When the dinosaurs died out, the climate of the world was changing. It was getting **colder**—and mammals had bodies that were **made to survive** in colder places.

During the many long years when they had to "hide out" from dinosaurs, mammals were **nocturnal animals.** To stay active at night and hunt their food, they developed bodies that were very good at **making and keeping heat.**

At the same time, mammals evolved new ways to **protect and feed their babies.** Instead of laying eggs, mammal mothers started to carry babies **inside their bodies.** And they began to stay with their babies after they were born. As a result, more babies survived.

Ⓑ

PROTECTED FROM COLD

As you remember, the ancestors of the mammals were **therapsids**—and they were probably **warm-blooded.** They could make heat inside their bodies by **metabolizing** (or "burning") food. Mammals inherited this ability **and improved it.**

Therapsids probably **had hair** on their bodies to **keep the heat inside.** And mammals inherited this, too. They could move around **in cold water** as a result.

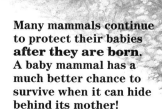

Many mammals continue to protect their babies **after they are born.** A baby mammal has a much better chance to survive when it can hide behind its mother!

As you know, **reptile eggs** offer some protection for the babies inside. But the mother leaves after she lays them Ⓐ. So **they are "helpless"** if a predator comes along and digs them up Ⓑ. There is nothing the mother can do to protect them.

HELPLESS EGG

PROTECTED BY MOTHER

PROTECTED EGG

Mammal mothers usually carry their eggs **inside their bodies** Ⓒ. This way, a mother can use **her size and strength** to protect her babies until they are born—and more babies survive as a result.

FED BY MOTHER

As you know, reptiles have to find their own food after they hatch. But mother mammals **feed their babies milk** after they are born. This also helps more babies to survive.

The teeth of mammals were another reason why they took over so many niches. Teeth are very important to the success of all animals. They are **the main tools** that animals use to gather and eat their food. Mammals were able to develop **a greater variety** of different tools in their mouths than other animals—so they were more successful.

Most mammals have **specialized teeth**—special teeth for eating special kinds of food. Insect-eating mammals have different teeth than plant-eating mammals. And meat-eating mammals have different teeth, too.

But all mammals **chew their food,** to release the maximum amount of energy from it. They need to do this because they are warm-blooded animals with **a high metabolism.** They must find and "burn" a lot of food to keep their body heat high—and **keep energy flowing** in their bodies.

PLANT-EATERS

There are two general types of plant-eating mammals. **Browsers** (BROW-zurs) eat the leaves, fruits, and nuts of plants.

During the Age of Dinosaurs, **all mammals ate insects.** They already had special teeth to do the job.

INSECT-EATERS

Insects are often **hard to grab** and **difficult to eat.** Many of them have shells that must be sliced open or crushed. Mammals had different teeth for **grabbing, slicing** and **crushing.**

In front of the mouth, there were long and sharp teeth that were used for **grabbing prey Ⓐ.** These teeth are called the **canines** (KAY-nines).

CANINES STAB PREY

INCISORS CUT

In front of the canines were teeth **for slicing Ⓑ**—the **incisors** (in-SIZE-urs). And behind the canines were teeth **for crushing Ⓒ**—the **cheek teeth.**

CHEEK TEETH CRUSH

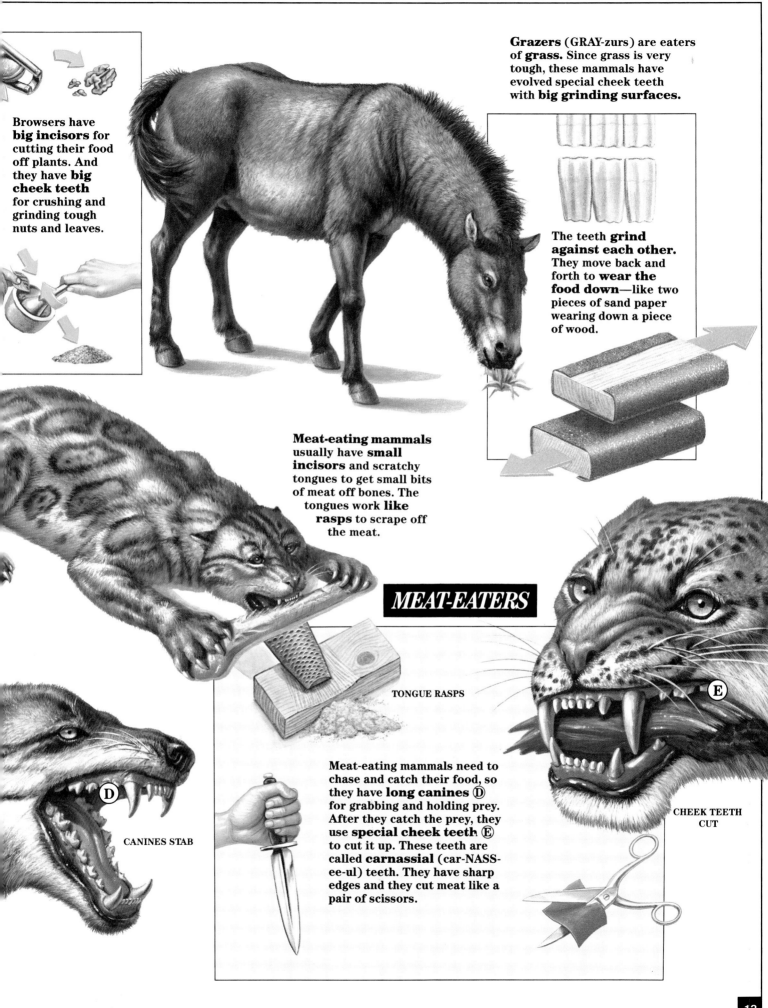

Browsers have **big incisors** for cutting their food off plants. And they have **big cheek teeth** for crushing and grinding tough nuts and leaves.

Grazers (GRAY-zurs) are eaters of **grass.** Since grass is very tough, these mammals have evolved special cheek teeth with **big grinding surfaces.**

The teeth **grind against each other.** They move back and forth to **wear the food down**—like two pieces of sand paper wearing down a piece of wood.

Meat-eating mammals usually have **small incisors** and scratchy tongues to get small bits of meat off bones. The tongues work **like rasps** to scrape off the meat.

MEAT-EATERS

TONGUE RASPS

CANINES STAB

D

Meat-eating mammals need to chase and catch their food, so they have **long canines** Ⓓ for grabbing and holding prey. After they catch the prey, they use **special cheek teeth** Ⓔ to cut it up. These teeth are called **carnassial** (car-NASS-ee-ul) teeth. They have sharp edges and they cut meat like a pair of scissors.

E

CHEEK TEETH CUT

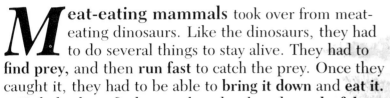

Meat-eating mammals took over from meat-eating dinosaurs. Like the dinosaurs, they had to do several things to stay alive. They **had to find prey,** and then **run fast** to catch the prey. Once they caught it, they had to be able to **bring it down** and **eat it.**

To help them find prey, they developed **wonderful senses**—hearing, sight and smell. To run faster, they evolved **longer legs.** And to bring prey down, they developed **strong muscles** and **sharp claws.** As you have seen, they also developed special teeth for grabbing and cutting.

FINDING PREY

EXCELLENT HEARING is needed to find prey in thick brush, or in the dark. Meat-eating mammals usually have **large ears** Ⓐ to help them hear better. They can **turn the ears** in many directions —to find out *exactly* where sounds are coming from.

Ⓐ

FINE EYESIGHT can often see prey at great distances. The eyes of meat-eating mammals are **side by side,** in front of the head—like your eyes. Like you, they can tell **how far away** things are. So they can decide if prey is close enough to catch.

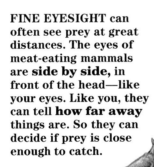

WON'T CATCH

MIGHT CATCH

EASY CATCH

SENSITIVE SMELL is used for tracking prey. Meat-eating mammals often have **long noses**—with plenty of room inside for lots of special tissues that "catch" smells.

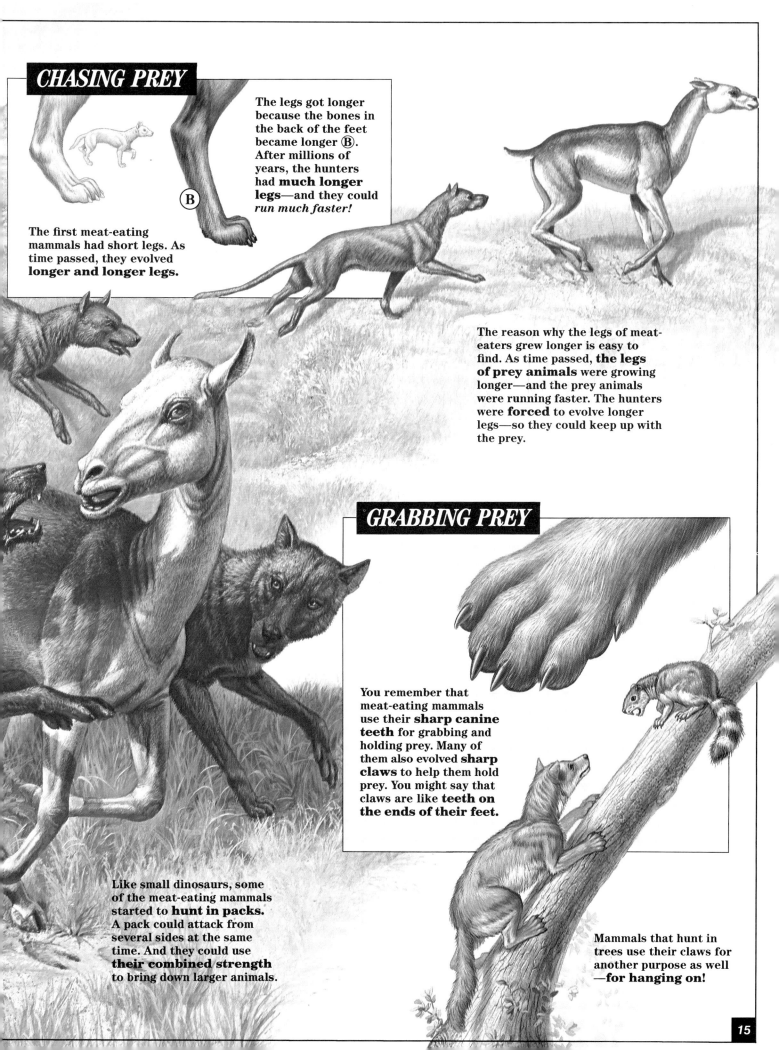

CHASING PREY

The first meat-eating mammals had short legs. As time passed, they evolved **longer and longer legs.**

The legs got longer because the bones in the back of the feet became longer Ⓑ. After millions of years, the hunters had **much longer legs**—and they could *run much faster!*

The reason why the legs of meat-eaters grew longer is easy to find. As time passed, **the legs of prey animals** were growing longer—and the prey animals were running faster. The hunters were **forced** to evolve longer legs—so they could keep up with the prey.

GRABBING PREY

You remember that meat-eating mammals use their **sharp canine teeth** for grabbing and holding prey. Many of them also evolved **sharp claws** to help them hold prey. You might say that claws are like **teeth on the ends of their feet.**

Like small dinosaurs, some of the meat-eating mammals started to **hunt in packs.** A pack could attack from several sides at the same time. And they could use **their combined strength** to bring down larger animals.

Mammals that hunt in trees use their claws for another purpose as well —**for hanging on!**

Dogs and bears look very different from each other today, but they are descended from **the same ancestors.** Over millions of years, their bodies evolved in different ways for them to lead different kinds of lives.

Dogs feed themselves by **chasing prey.** To do this, they evolved **longer legs** and started to hunt in packs. Bears can kill prey, but they also **eat a lot of plant food**—so they have large bodies, with **big stomachs.**

By studying fossils and the bones of living animals, scientists have discovered that **badgers and raccoons** are also related to dogs and bears.

The ancestors of both dogs and bears were primitive mammals that lived about 60 million years ago.

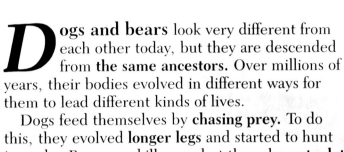

They had **short legs, and probably hunted small prey in the forest.**

WILD DOGS

The legs of dogs got longer, so they could run faster. Dogs started to run **on their toes.**

The teeth of dogs became more and more specialized for **eating meat.**

The wild dogs of today are the end result of this line of evolution. They are intelligent animals that often live and hunt in family groups or packs. The finest example is probably the wolf—the ancestor of all domestic dogs.

BADGERS & WEASELS

Badgers and weasels look like their primitive ancestors in some ways—and they live similar lives. **They hunt small prey** in the forest.

The teeth of bears and raccoons evolved to eat **meat and plants.** The cheek teeth of bears are good for crushing plant food.

RACCOONS

Raccoons can eat **almost anything**—and this is one reason why they are very successful mammals.

BEARS

PLANT FOOD

To carry all the bulky plant food they eat, bears need **big stomachs.** And they need **big bodies** to carry the big stomachs. Of course, big bodies are also useful for killing big prey.

To support the heavy weight of their large bodies, bears must walk **on flat feet.** But they can still run fast when they want to.

Cats and hyenas are descended from *the same group* of primitive meat-eating mammals as dogs and bears. Like dogs and bears, the cats and the hyenas evolved **to fill different niches.** They get their food in different ways—and they have different bodies and teeth to do it.

Cats usually hunt alone and sneak up on their prey. Hyenas often hunt in groups, chasing their prey like dogs. They also **scavenge**—eating the remains of dead animals that other predators have killed.

Cats started to evolve from their primitive ancestors about 40 million years ago. The first hyenas appeared about 20 million years ago.

HYENAS

Like dogs, hyenas evolved longer and longer legs, to run faster. As time passed, their bodies grew **larger and stronger** —so they could bring down larger prey.

Hyenas like to eat **the marrow** that is found inside bones. To get marrow, they must break open the bones—and they have **special heavy teeth** for crushing bone.

BIG & LITTLE CATS

All cats living today use their canine teeth like daggers **to stab** their prey. They try to surprise the prey and kill it quickly, with one bite of the canines.

Soon after cats started to evolve, one group developed **very long canine teeth.** These became the famous sabre-tooth cats.

SABRE-TOOTH CATS

...ike meat-eating dinosaurs, ...abre-tooth cats had **serrated** ...dges on their huge canines. ...his made it easier for the teeth ...o cut into prey.

EMPTY NICHE

When reptiles died out in the sea, they left empty niches . . .

M ammals that live in the sea are descended from mammals that lived **on the land**. Strange as it may seem, animals like porpoises and whales are descended from animals that probably looked like **small, hairy dogs!**

When the dinosaurs died out, the marine reptiles also became extinct—and they left **many empty niches** in the sea. Some land mammals went back into the water to fill some of these niches.

The ancestors of porpoises and whales were probably land animals that hunted for food at the edge of the sea.

PORPOISE ANCESTOR

NEW TAILS & FINS

The mammals grew **broad tails** Ⓓ to push them through the water—and **fins on their backs** Ⓔ to help them swim straight.

Ⓔ

③

Ⓓ

After the dangerous reptiles died out, the mammals could start hunting **in the water.**

THEIR BODIES CHANGED

As time passed, they spent **more and more time** in the water. Their bodies changed so they could swim better and catch food more easily.

Ⓑ

Ⓐ

①

Over millions of years, the front legs **flattened out** until they looked like the pectoral fins of fish Ⓐ. The back legs were lost Ⓑ.

Ⓒ

②

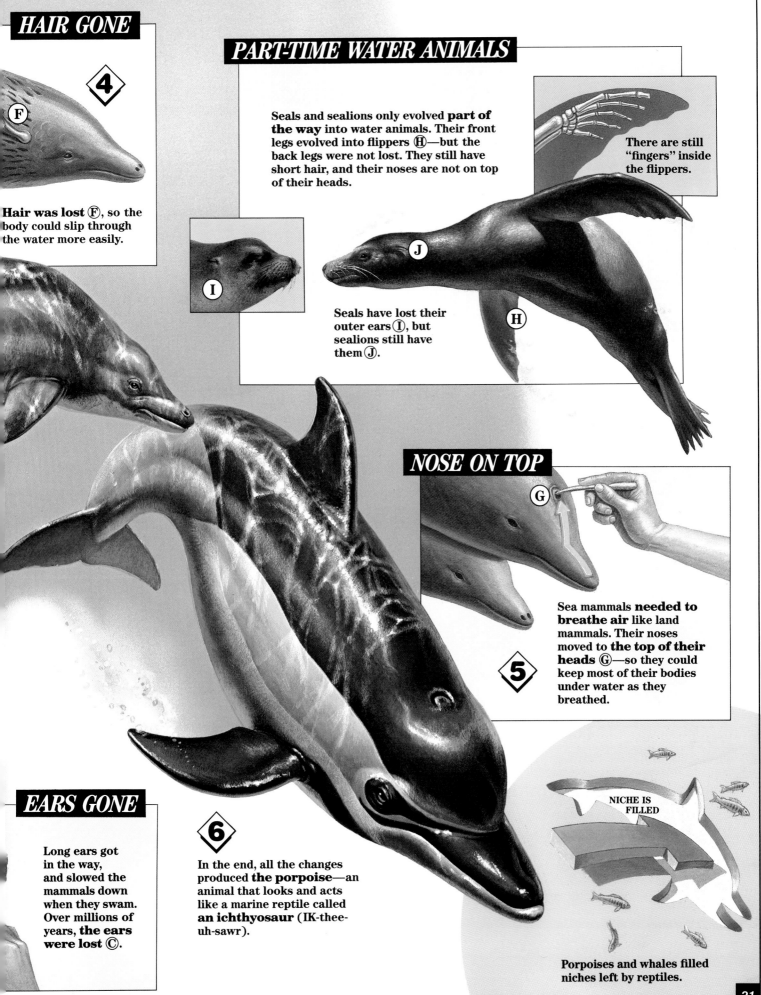

HAIR GONE

④ Ⓕ

Hair was lost Ⓕ, so the body could slip through the water more easily.

PART-TIME WATER ANIMALS

Seals and sealions only evolved **part of the way** into water animals. Their front legs evolved into flippers Ⓗ—but the back legs were not lost. They still have short hair, and their noses are not on top of their heads.

There are still "fingers" inside the flippers.

Ⓙ

Ⓘ

Ⓗ

Seals have lost their outer ears Ⓘ, but sealions still have them Ⓙ.

NOSE ON TOP

Ⓖ

⑤ Sea mammals **needed to breathe air** like land mammals. Their noses moved to **the top of their heads** Ⓖ—so they could keep most of their bodies under water as they breathed.

EARS GONE

Long ears got in the way, and slowed the mammals down when they swam. Over millions of years, **the ears were lost** Ⓒ.

⑥ In the end, all the changes produced **the porpoise**—an animal that looks and acts like a marine reptile called **an ichthyosaur** (IK-thee-uh-sawr).

NICHE IS FILLED

Porpoises and whales filled niches left by reptiles.

REMEMBER:

1 When the dinosaurs and the marine reptiles died out, they left **many empty niches** on land and in the water. Over millions of years, **many new mammals** evolved to fill the niches.

2 The world was getting colder when the dinosaurs died—and mammals had special bodies that could live in the cold. For one thing, **they could make heat** inside their bodies— and **they had hair** to keep the heat in.

3 Mammals also did more to **take care of their babies.** Reptile mothers laid eggs and then left them—so predators could dig them up. The eggs were rather "helpless."

4 Mammal mothers carried their babies around **inside their bodies** until the babies were born. This way, a mother could use her own size and strength to protect her babies better.

5 Mammals also had **specialized teeth.** They had **incisors** to cut food, **canines** to grab and hold prey—and **cheek teeth** for crushing and grinding.

6 Meat-eating mammals and plant-eating mammals developed different kinds of teeth. And plant-eaters were divided into **browsers** and **grazers.**

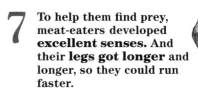

7 To help them find prey, meat-eaters developed **excellent senses.** And their **legs got longer** and longer, so they could run faster.

8 The meat-eaters had to run faster and faster because their prey was running faster and faster. They were **forced to evolve** longer legs.

9 To grab prey, meat-eating mammals evolved long canine teeth and **sharp claws.**

NEW WORDS:

Canine Teeth

(KAY-nine):
Long, sharp teeth that meat-eating mammals use for grabbing and holding prey. They are also used for stabbing.

Incisor Teeth

(in-SIZE-ur):
Small teeth in front of the mouth that are used to cut food. Meat-eating mammals use them to get bits of meat off bones.

Browsers

(BROW-zurs):
Plant-eating mammals that eat mostly leaves and other parts of bushes and trees.

10 The niches that meat-eating mammals filled determined what their bodies looked like. Dogs started to chase prey—and their legs got longer to help them run faster.

11 Bears filled niches where they ate meat and plants. They evolved large stomachs to hold bulky plant food—and large bodies to carry the stomachs.

12 Hyenas evolved to chase prey like dogs—but also **to scavenge** animals killed by other predators. They evolved long legs for running and **heavy teeth** for cracking open bones.

13 Cats sneak up on prey and try to kill it with one bite of their large canine teeth. Sabretooth cats evolved **huge canines** for stabbing large animals.

14 Mammals that live in the sea are descended from land mammals. When marine reptiles died out, some land mammals started to go **into the water** to find food.

15 As time passed they spent more and more time in the water—and **their bodies changed** to make it easier for them to move in water.

Grazers

(GRAY-zurs):
Plant-eating mammals that eat mostly grass. They have very large cheek teeth for grinding up their tough food.

Carnassial Teeth

(car-NASS-ee-ul):
Special cheek teeth that some meat-eating mammals have. Used to cut up meat before it is swallowed.

Ichthyosaur

(IK-thee-uh-sawr):
Ancient marine reptile that died out when the dinosaurs became extinct. One of the reptiles that left niches that were filled by sea mammals.

Index